THE SECRET OF THE
FAITH LIFE

THE SECRET OF THE
FAITH LIFE

Andrew Murray

PUBLICATIONS

Fort Washington, PA 19034

The Secret of the Faith Life
Published by CLC Publications

U.S.A.
P.O. Box 1449, Fort Washington, PA 19034

UNITED KINGDOM
CLC International (UK)
Unit 5, Glendale Avenue, Sandycroft, Flintshire, CH5 2QP

Printed in the United States of America

ISBN (trade paper): 978-1-61958-270-5
ISBN (e-book): 978-1-61958-271-2

Unless otherwise noted, all Scripture quotations are from the Holy Bible, New King James Version, copyright © 1979, 1980, 1982 by Thomas Nelson, Inc. Used by permission. All rights reserved.

Italics in Scripture quotations are the emphasis of the author.

Cover design by Mitch Bolton.

A PRAYER

I ASKED of God, "Give me a word
Of power, that mortals never heard,
That through the earth like flame shall fly
And quicken souls that sleeping lie.
The old words are outworn, that long
On banners flamed, or throbbed in song.
Love traffics, faith is in eclipse,
And silent are the prophet's lips.
Some new great word of thrilling tone
From out the choirs of heaven loan,
That I may cry it through the earth
Till faith and love shall have new birth."

Then waiting in the silence dim
Where dwelt the dreadful cherubim,
I felt a voice say, low and deep:
"The old words still their power keep.
Cry them again, and cry, and cry,
The human heart shall give reply.
There are in all the heaven above
No mightier words than *Faith* and *Love*."

EVER-BLESSED God and Father, how shall we praise You aright for that wonderful salvation which You have prepared for us in Christ Jesus!

We humbly confess that we have so little understood it, believed it, yielded ourselves to its power, and so little shown forth its beauty to the world around. Most fervently do we pray for all saints that You would give them a vision of the abundant life there is in Christ Jesus. May that stir their hearts to a deep unquenchable longing to know fully what Christ is meant to be to them. May they feel deeply how all the impotence of Your church to bless the world is owing to nothing but this—not giving Christ and His Holy Spirit the place in their hearts that You would have.

And grant, above all, such an insight into the need, into the power, into the blessedness of a simple whole-hearted faith in Jesus Christ, and an unreserved surrender to His mastery, that their hearts may be prepared to receive Him in all the fullness of His love and of His abiding presence.

Our Father, we beseech You, hear us in the name of Jesus, and give to each reader of this little book such a sight of Your power to fulfill in us every promise, and such a humble childlike trust in Your faithfulness as will be to Your glory.
And to You be all the glory for ever and ever.

AMEN.

Day 1

The Image of God

Then God said, "Let Us make man in Our image, according to Our likeness."

Genesis 1:26

HERE we have the first thought of man—his origin and his destiny entirely divine. God undertook the stupendous work of making a creature, who is not God, to be a perfect likeness of Him in His divine glory. Man was to live in entire dependence on God, and to receive directly and unceasingly from Him the inflow of all that was holy and blessed in the Divine Being. God's glory, His holiness and His love, were to dwell in him, and shine out through him.

When sin had done its terrible work and spoiled the image of God, the promise was given in Paradise of the seed of the woman, in whom the divine purpose would be fulfilled. "[God's Son,] the brightness of His glory and the express image of His person" (Heb. 1:3), was to become a Son of man, in whom God's plan would be carried out, His image revealed in human form. The New Testament takes up the thought of creation and speaks of those who are "predestined to be conformed to the image of His Son" (Rom. 8:29); of "the new man . . . renewed . . . according to the image of Him who created him" (Col. 3:10); and gives the promise: "We know that when He is revealed, we shall be like Him, for we shall see Him as He is" (1 John 3:2).

And, between the eternal purpose and its eternal realization, we have a wonderful promise in regard to the life here upon earth: "We all . . . beholding . . . the glory of the Lord, are being transformed into the same image from glory to glory, just as by the Spirit of the Lord" (2 Cor. 3:18).

It was of this that Paul had said just before: "how will the ministry of the Spirit not be more glorious?" (3:8). Let us take home the promise of the text as the possible and assured experience for daily life to every one who gives Christ His place as the Glorified One. Let us keep the heart set upon the glory of that image of God in Christ, in the assurance that the Spirit will change us into the same image day by day, from glory to glory. O my soul, take time to believe firmly and confidently that this promise will be made true in thy Christian life. God Almighty, who created man in His image, seeks now to work out His purpose in changing you into the image of Christ Jesus by the power of the Holy Spirit.

"Let this mind be in you which was also in Christ Jesus" (Phil. 2:5). "I have given you an example, that you should do as I have done to you" (John 13:15).

"[Lord], increase our faith" (Luke 17:5).

The Obedience of Faith

The LORD appeared to Abram and said to him, "I am Almighty God; walk before Me and be blameless. And I will make My covenant between Me and you, and will multiply you exceedingly."

Genesis 17:1–2

IN Abraham we see how God not only asks for faith, and rewards faith, but also how He works faith by the gracious training that He gives. When God first called him, He at once gave the great promise, "In you all the families of the earth shall be blessed" (12:3). When he reached the land, God met him with the promise that the land should be his (see 12:7). When Abraham returned from the battle against the kings, God again met him to renew the promise (see 15:5). Before the birth of Isaac, in the words of our text, He sought to strengthen his faith (see chapter 17). And once more, in the plains of Mamre, He spoke: "Is anything too hard for the LORD?" (18:14). Step by step God led him until his faith was perfected for full obedience in the sacrifice of Isaac. As "by faith Abraham obeyed when he was called to go out" (Heb. 11:8), so by faith, at the close of forty years, he was able, without any promise, in fact in apparent conflict with all the promises, to obey God's will to the very uttermost.

Children of Abraham, children of God, the Father

makes great demands on your faith. If you are to follow in Abraham's footsteps, you too are to forsake all, to live in the land of spiritual promise with nothing but His word to depend upon, separated unto God. For this you will need a deep and clear insight that the God who is working in you is the Almighty who will work all His good pleasure. Do not think that it is a little thing and easy to live the life of faith. It calls for a life that seeks to abide in His presence all the day. Bow before God in humble worship until He speaks to you too: "I am Almighty God; walk before Me and be blameless. . . . And I will . . . multiply you exceedingly" (Gen 17:1–2). When Abraham heard this, he "fell on his face, and God talked with him" (17:3). There you have the secret birthplace of the power to trust God for everything that He promises.

In this little book we desire to find out both what the power of faith is and what God is willing to work, "what is the exceeding greatness of His power toward us who believe" (Eph. 1:19). So we can go out like Abraham only when we are called to a life of true consecration to God and of the obedience of faith to the very uttermost. Walk in the footsteps of Abraham. Hide deep in your heart the testimony of God's Word: "[He] was strengthened in faith, giving glory to God, and being fully convinced that what He had promised He was also able to perform" (Rom. 4:20–21).

The Love of God

You shall love the LORD your God with all your heart, with all your soul, and with all your strength.

Deuteronomy 6:5

GOD taught Abraham what it was to *believe in God with all his heart*; he was strong in faith, giving glory to God. Moses taught Israel what the first and great commandment was: *to love God with all your heart*. This was the first commandment as the origin and fountain out of which the others naturally proceed. It has its ground in the relationship between God as the *loving* Creator and man made in His image as the object of that love. In the very nature of things it could never be otherwise: man finds his life, his destiny, and his happiness in nothing but just this one thing, *loving God with all the heart and all the strength*. Moses said: "The LORD delighted only in your fathers, to love them" (10:15); such a God was infinitely worthy of being loved. All our religion, all our faith in God and obedience to Him, our *whole life* is to be inspired by the one thought: *We are to love God with all our heart and all our strength*. Every day the child of God has as his first duty to live out this command.

How little Israel was able to obey the command we all know well. But before Moses died, he was able, after speaking of the judgments God would bring upon His people for their sins, to make known this promise: "the

Lᴏʀᴅ your God will circumcise your heart"—with a circumcision not made with hands, but the circumcision of Christ on the cross (see Col. 2:11)—"to love the Lᴏʀᴅ your God with all your heart and with all your soul"(Deut. 30:6).

This blessed promise was the first indication of the new covenant, in which Jeremiah foretold of the law so written in the heart by the Holy Spirit that they should no more depart from God but walk in His ways. But how little have Christians understood this; how easily they rest content with the thought that it is impossible.

Let us learn the double lesson. This perfect heart, loving God with all our might, is what God claims, is what God is infinitely worthy of, is what God—blessed be His name!—*will Himself give and work in us*. Let our whole soul go out in faith to meet, to wait for, and to expect the fulfillment of the promise that to love God with the whole heart is what God Himself will work in us.

"The love of God has been poured out in our hearts by the Holy Spirit who was given to us" (Rom. 5:5). That makes the grace of loving God with all our heart most sure and blessed.

The Joyful Sound

Blessed are the people who know the joyful sound! They walk, O Lord, in the light of Your countenance. In Your name they rejoice all day long.

Psalm 89:15–16

"GOOD tidings of great joy" (Luke 2:10) was what the angel calls the gospel message. This is what is here spoken of as "the joyful sound." That blessedness consists in God's people walking in the light of God and rejoicing in His name all the day. Undisturbed fellowship, never-ending joy, is their portion. Even in the Old Testament such was at times the experience of the saints. But there was no continuance; the old covenant could not secure that. Only the new covenant can and does give it.

In every well-ordered family one finds the father delighting in his children, and the children rejoicing in their father's presence. And this mark of a happy home on earth is what the heavenly Father has promised and delights to work in His people: *walking in the light of His countenance and rejoicing in His name all the day.* It has been promised. It has been made possible in Christ through the Holy Spirit filling the heart with the love of God. It is the heritage of all who are seeking indeed to love God with all their heart and all their strength. And yet how many there are of God's children who simply think it impossible and have even given up the hope, the desire, for a life of rejoicing in God's presence all the day. And yet Christ promised it so definitely: "These things I have spoken to you, that My joy may remain in you, and that your joy may be full" (John 15:11). "I will see you again and your heart will rejoice, and your joy no one will take from you" (16:22).

Let us think of the Father's longing to have the perfect confidence and love of His children, and of the children's need of the Father's presence every moment of the day for their happiness and strength. Let us think of the power of Christ by the Holy Spirit to maintain this life in us; and let us be content with nothing less than the blessedness of them that know the joyful sound: "They walk, O LORD, in the light of Your countenance. In Your name they rejoice all day long . . . for You are the glory of their strength" (Ps. 89:15-17).

The deeper we seek to enter into God's will for us, the stronger our faith will be that the Father can be content with nothing less than this: His child walking in the light of His countenance and rejoicing in His name all the day; and the stronger will the assurance come that what the Father has meant for us will be wrought in us through Christ and the Holy Spirit. Let us just hold fast the word—*all the day, all the day*.

Day 5

The Thoughts of God

As the heavens are higher than the earth, so are My ways higher than your thoughts.

Isaiah 55:9

IN giving us His promises of what He will work in us, God reminds us that as high as the heavens are above the earth, so high His thoughts are above ours—altogether beyond our power of spiritual living apprehension.

When He tells us that we are made in the image of God, that by grace we are actually renewed again into that image, and as we gaze upon God's glory in Christ we are changed into the same image as by the Spirit of the Lord—this is indeed a thought higher than the heavens. When He tells Abraham of all the mighty work He was to do in him, and in his seed, and through him in all the nations of the earth, that again is a thought higher than the heavens—man's mind could not take it in. When God calls us to love Him with all our heart, and promises to renew our hearts so that they shall love Him with all our strength, that again is a thought out of the very heights of heaven. And when the Father calls us to a life here on earth in the light of His face and rejoicing in His name all the day, we have a gift out of the very depths of God's heart of love.

What deep reverence and humility and patience become us in waiting upon God by His Holy Spirit, to impart to our hearts the life and the light that can make us feel at home with these thoughts dwelling in us. What need of daily, tender, abiding fellowship with God if we are in very deed to enter into His mind and to have His thoughts make their home in us. And what a faith especially is needed to believe that God will not only reveal the beauty and the glory of these thoughts, but will actually so mightily work in us that their divine reality and blessing shall indeed fill our inmost being.

Just think of what Isaiah says, as quoted by Paul (1 Cor. 2:9–10): "Eye has not seen, nor ear heard, nor have entered into the heart of man the things which God has prepared for those who love Him. But God has revealed them to us through His Spirit." When Christ promised His disciples that the Holy Spirit from the throne in heaven was to dwell with them, He said that the Spirit who would glorify Him would fill us with the light and life of the heavenly world. It was *that* that would make Him and the purposes of God, higher than the heavens above the earth their abiding experience. O my soul, seek to realize that every day the Holy Spirit will fill your heart with the thoughts of God in all their heavenly power and glory.

The New Covenant in Jeremiah 31

*I will make a new covenant with the house of Israel. . . . I
will put My law in their minds, and write it on their hearts.*
Jeremiah 31:31, 33

WHEN God made the first covenant with Israel
at Sinai, He said, "If you will indeed obey My
voice and keep My covenant, then you shall be a special
treasure to Me above all people" (Exod. 19:5). But Israel,
alas, had not the power to obey. Their whole nature was
carnal and sinful. In the covenant there was no provision
for the grace that should make them obedient. The law
only served to show them their sin.

In our text God promises to make a new covenant
in which provision would be made to enable men to live
a life of obedience. In this new covenant, the law was to
be put in their inward parts and written in their heart,
"not with ink but *by the Spirit of the living God*" (2 Cor.
3:3), so that they could say with David: "I delight to do
Your will, O my God, and Your law is within my heart"
(Ps. 40:8). The law, and delight in it, would, through
the Holy Spirit, take possession of the inner life with all
its powers. Or, as we have it in Jeremiah, after God had
said "Is there anything too hard for Me?" (32:27): "I
will make an everlasting covenant with them . . . I will
put My fear in their hearts so that they will not depart
from Me" (32:40).

In contrast with the old testament and its weakness, which made it impossible to continue faithful, this promise ensures a continual, whole-hearted obedience as the mark of the believer who takes God at His word and fully claims what the promise secures.

Learn the lesson that in the new covenant God's mighty power will be shown in the heart of everyone who believes the promise: "They will not depart from Me." "I believe God that it will be just as it was told me" (Acts 27:25). Bow in deep stillness before God and believe what He says. The measure of our experience of this power of God keeping us from departing from Him will ever be in harmony with the law: "*According to your faith let it be to you*" (Matt. 9:29).

We need to be at great pains to keep the contrast between the Old and the New Testament very clear. The Old had a wonderful measure of grace, but not enough for the continual abiding in the faith of obedience. That is the definite promise of the New Testament, the fruit of heart renewal and the power of the Holy Spirit leading the soul and revealing the fullness of grace to keep us "blameless in holiness" (1 Thess. 3:13).

The New Covenant in Ezekiel

I will sprinkle clean water on you, and you shall be clean; I will cleanse you from all your filthiness. . . . I will put My Spirit within you and cause you to walk in My statutes, and you will keep My judgments.

Ezekiel 36:25, 27

HERE we have the same promise as in Jeremiah, the promise of such a heart cleansing from sin, and such a gift of the Spirit in the new heart, as would secure their walking in His statutes and keeping His judgments. Just as in Jeremiah God had said: "I will put My law in their minds, and write it on their hearts. . . . I will put My fear in their hearts so that they will not depart from Me" (Jer. 31:33; 32:40), so here: "I will . . . cause you to walk in My statutes, and you will keep My judgments" (Ezek. 36:27). In contrast with the old covenant, in which there was no power to enable them to continue in God's law, the great mark of the new covenant would be a divine power enabling them to walk in His statutes and keep His judgments.

"Where sin abounded, grace abounded much more" (Rom. 5:20), working whole-hearted allegiance and obedience. Why is this so little experienced? The answer is very simple: The promise is not believed, is not preached; its fulfillment is not expected. And yet how clearly we have it in a passage like Romans 8:1–4. There the man who had complained of the power "bringing [him] into captivity to the law of sin" (Rom. 7:23) thanks God that he is "now . . . in Christ Jesus" (8:1); and that "the law of the Spirit of life in Christ Jesus has made [him] free from the law of sin and death" (8:2), so that the requirement of the law is fulfilled in all who walk after the Spirit.

Once again, why are there so few who can give such testimony and declare what is to be done to attain to it? Just one thing is needed—the faith in an omnipotent God who will by His wonderful power do what He has promised: "*I, the L*ORD*, have spoken it . . . and I will do it*" (Ezek. 24:14). Oh, let us begin to believe that the promise will come true: "You shall be clean; I will cleanse you from all your filthiness. . . . [I will] cause you to walk in My statutes, and you will keep My judgments." Let us believe all that God here promises and God will do it. To an extent beyond all power of thought, God has made His great and glorious promises dependent on our faith! And the promises will build that faith as we believe them. "According to your faith let it be to you" (Matt. 9:29). Let us this very day put it to the proof.

The New Covenant and Prayer

Call to Me, and I will answer you, and show you great and mighty things, which you do not know.

Jeremiah 33:3

I, the LORD, have spoken it, and I will do it. . . . I will also let the house of Israel inquire of Me to do this for them.

Ezekiel 36:36–37

THE fulfillment of the great promises of the new covenant is made dependent on prayer. In answer to the prayer of Jeremiah, God had said: "I will put My fear in their hearts so that they will not depart from Me" (Jer. 32:40). And to Ezekiel He had spoken: " I will . . . cause you to walk in My statutes, and you will keep My judgments" (36:27). To us in our unbelief, and our judging of the meaning of God's Word according to human thought and experience, there is no expectation of these promises being truly fulfilled. We do not believe that God means them to be literally true. We have not the faith in the mighty power of God that is waiting to make His promise true in our experience.

And God has said that without such faith our experience will be but very partial and very limited. He has graciously pointed out the way in which such faith can be found. It is in the path of much prayer. *"Call to Me, and I will answer you, and show you great and mighty things, which you do not know." "I will also let the house of Israel inquire of Me to do this for them."* It is when individual men and women turn to God with their whole heart to plead these promises that He will fulfill them. It is in the exercise of intense persevering prayer that faith will be strengthened to take hold of God and surrender itself to His omnipotent working. And then, as one and another can testify of what God has done and will do, believers will help each other and take their place as the church of the living God, pleading for and firmly expecting that His promises will be fulfilled in larger measure as a new enduement for the great work of preaching Christ in the fullness of His redemption to perishing men.

The state of the church, the state of our ministers and members, our own state calls for unceasing prayer. We need to pray intensely and persistently that the need of the power of the Holy Spirit may be deeply felt, and that a strong faith may be roused in the hearts of many to claim and to expect His mighty working. "I, the Lord, have spoken it . . . and I will do it" (Ezek. 24:14).

"Lord, I believe; help my unbelief!" (Mark 9:24).

The New Covenant in Hebrews

For I will be merciful to their unrighteousness, and their sins . . . I will remember no more.

Hebrews 8:12

CHRIST is called in this epistle the Mediator of a better covenant, enacted upon better promises (see 8:6). In Him the two parts of the covenant find their complete fulfillment. First of all, He came to atone for sin, so that its power over man was destroyed and free access to God's presence and favor was secured. And with that came the fuller blessing, the new heart, freed from the power of sin, with God's Holy Spirit breathing into it the delight in God's law and the power to obey it.

These two parts of the covenant may never be separated. And yet, alas, how many there are who put their trust in Christ for the forgiveness of sin and yet never think of claiming the fullness of the promise—the new heart cleansed from sin, with the Holy Spirit breathing in it such love and delight in God's law, and such power to obey, that they have access to the full blessing of the new covenant, being God's people and knowing Him as their God.

Jesus Christ is "the Mediator of the new covenant" (Heb. 9:15), with the forgiveness of sin in the power of His blood and the law written in the heart in the power of His Spirit. Oh that we could understand that just as surely as the complete pardon of sin is assured, the complete fulfillment of the promises, "I will put My fear in their hearts so that they will not depart from Me" (Jer. 32:40) and " I will . . . cause you to walk in My statutes, and you will keep My judgments" (36:27), may be expected too.

But remember what God said to Abraham: "I am Almighty God. . . . Is anything too hard for the LORD?" (Gen. 17:1; 18:14). He spoke that word to Jeremiah too, in regard to the new covenant. This calls for strong, whole-hearted desire for a life wholly given up to Him. It involves a setting aside of all our preconceived opinions and in faith, believing in the mighty power of God; a surrender to Jesus Christ as the Mediator of the new covenant, willing to accept our place with Him, crucified to the world, to sin and to self. It means a readiness to follow Him at any cost. In one word, it means a simple, whole-hearted acceptance of Christ as Lord and Master, heart and life wholly His. God has said it and will do it. "I, the LORD, have spoken it . . . and I will do it" (Ezek. 24:14).

Day 10

The Trial of Faith

And [Naaman's] servants came near and spoke to him, and said, "My father, if the prophet had told you to do something great, would you not have done it? How much more then, when he says to you, 'Wash, and be clean'?"

Second Kings 5:13

IN Naaman we have a striking Old Testament illustration of the place faith takes in God's dealing with man. It gives us a wonderful revelation of what faith really is. Think first of how intense the desire was for healing on Naaman's part. He would do anything—appeal to the King of Syria and the King of Israel; he would undertake a long journey and humble himself before the prophet, who did not even deign to come out and see him. In this intensity of desire for blessing we have the root of a strong faith. And it is just this seeking for God and His blessing which is too much lacking in our religion.

The second mark of faith is that it has to give up all its preconceived opinions and to bow before the word of God. This was more than Naaman was willing to do, and he turned away in a rage. It was well for him that a wise and faithful servant gave him better advice. Faith is often held back by the question of how such a simple thing as to accept God's word can effect such a mighty revolution in the heart.

And then comes the third mark of faith. It submits implicitly to the word of God: "Wash, and be clean." At first all appears vain, but faith proves itself in obedience. It does it not once or twice but seven times in the assurance that the mighty wonder will be wrought. It takes the simple word, "Wash, and be clean," and lo, it finds itself renewed as with the life of a little child, "completely clean" (John 13:10). The mighty deed is done.

When God's Word brings us to the promise: "I will sprinkle clean water on you, and you shall be clean; I will cleanse you from all your filthiness" (Ezek. 36:25), it is nothing but unbelief that holds us back. Let us believe that a simple, determined surrender of the whole will to God's promise will indeed bring the heart-cleansing we need. "There is a river whose streams shall make glad the city of God" (Ps. 46:4). It flows from under the throne of God and the Lamb, through the channels of a thousand precious promises; and at each step the word is heard: "Wash, and be clean." Christ cleanses "with the washing of water by the word" (Eph. 5:26). Every promise is a call: "Wash, and be clean; wash, and be clean"; and Christ will speak: "You are already clean because of the word which I have spoken to you" (John 15:3)—*completely clean*.

Faith in Christ

You believe in God, believe also in Me.

John 14:1

IN the Farewell Discourse (see John 14–17), when Christ was about to leave His disciples, He taught them that they were to believe in Him with the same perfect confidence which they had reposed in God. "You believe in God, *believe also in Me.*" "*Believe Me* that I am in the Father" (14:11). "*He who believes in Me, the works that I do he will do also*" (14:12). Here on earth He had not been able to make Himself fully known to His disciples. But in heaven the fullness of God's power would be His; and He would, in and through His disciples, do greater things than He had ever done upon earth. This faith must fix itself first of all on the person of Christ in His union with the Father. They were to have the perfect confidence that all that God had done could now be done by Jesus too. The deity of Christ is the rock on which our faith depends. Christ as man, partaker of our nature, is in very deed true God. As the divine power has worked in Christ even to the resurrection from the dead, so Christ can also, in His divine omnipotence, work in us all that we need.

Dear Christians, do you not see of what deep importance it is that you take time to worship Jesus in His divine omnipotence as one with the Father? That will teach you to count on Him in His sufficiency to work in us all that we can desire. This faith must so possess us that every thought of Christ will be filled with the consciousness of His presence as an almighty Redeemer, able to save and sanctify and empower us to the very uttermost.

Child of God, bow in deep humility before this blessed Lord Jesus and worship Him: my Lord and my God! Take time until you come under the full consciousness of an assured faith that as the almighty God, Christ will work for you, and in you and through you, all that God desires and all that you can need. Let the Savior you have known and loved become as never before the *mighty God*. Let Him be your confidence and your strength.

The Savior was about to leave the world. In His Farewell Charge on the last night He begins by telling them that everything would depend, through their whole life, on simply believing Him. By that faith they would do even greater things than He had ever done. And at the close of His address He repeats again: "Be of good cheer, I have overcome the world" (John 16:33). Our one need is a direct, definite, unceasing faith in the mighty power of Christ working in us.

Christ's Life in Us

Because I live, you will live also.

John 14:19

THERE is a great difference in the teaching of the three first Evangelists and that of John. John was the bosom friend of Jesus. He could understand the Master better than the others, and has recorded Christ's farewell teaching, of which they say nothing. This makes John 13–17 the inmost sanctuary of the new covenant. The others could speak of repentance and the pardon of sin as the first great gift of the New Testament. But of the new life which the new covenant was to bring, with the new heart in which the law had been put as a living power, they say little. It is, John records, what Christ taught about His very own life really becoming *ours*, and about our being united with Him just as He was with the Father. The other Evangelists speak of Christ as the Shepherd seeking and saving the lost. John speaks of Him as the Shepherd who so gives His life for the sheep that His very life becomes theirs. "I have come that they may have life, and that they may have *it* more abundantly" (10:10).

And so Christ says here, "Because I live, you will live also" (14:19). The disciples were to receive from Him not the life He then had, but the resurrection life in the power of its victory over death and the efficacy of His exaltation to the right hand of God. He would from thenceforth ever dwell in them—a new, a heavenly, an eternal life; the life of Jesus Himself would fill them. And this promise is to all who will accept it in faith.

Alas, how many there are who are content with the beginnings of the Christian life and never long to have it in its fullness, the more abundant life! They do not believe in it; they are not ready for the sacrifice implied in being wholly filled with the life of Jesus. Child of God, the message comes again to you: "*The things which are impossible with men are possible with God*" (Luke 18:27). I pray you, do take time, and let Christ's wonderful promise take possession of your heart. Be content with nothing less than a full salvation: *Christ living in you and you living in Christ.* Be assured that it is meant for everyone who will take time to listen to Christ's promises and who will believe that the almighty power of God will work in him the mighty wonder of His grace—Christ dwelling in the heart by faith.

The Obedience of Love

If you keep My commandments, you will abide in My love.
John 15:10

THE question is often asked: How can I come to abide in Christ always? To live wholly for Him?—such is my desire and fervent prayer. In our text the Lord gives the simple but far-reaching answer: "Keep My commandments." This is the only, the sure, the blessed way of abiding in Him. "If you keep My commandments, you will abide in My love, just as I have kept My Father's commandments and abide in His love." Loving obedience is the way to the enjoyment of His love.

Notice how often the Lord speaks of this in the last night. "If you love Me, keep My commandments" (14:15). And then again twice over: "He who has My commandments and keeps them, it is he who loves Me. And he who loves Me will be loved by My Father, and I will love him" (14:22). "If anyone loves Me, he will keep My word; and My Father will love him, and We will come to him and make Our home with him" (14:23). And so also thrice in chapter 15: "If . . . My words abide in you, you will ask what you desire, and it shall be done for you" (15:7). "If you keep My commandments, you will abide in My love" (15:10). "You are My friends if you do whatever I command you" (15:14). Six times over the Lord connects the keeping of the commandments with loving Him, and with the promise of the great blessing following on it, the indwelling of the Father and the Son in the heart. The love that keeps His commandments is the only way to abide in His love. In our whole relation to Christ, love is everything; Christ's love to us, our love to Him, proved in our love to the brethren.

How little have believers accepted this teaching. How content many are with the thought that it is impossible. They do not believe that through the grace of God we can be kept from sin. They do not believe in the promise of the new covenant (Ezek. 36:27): "I will put My Spirit within you *and cause you to walk in My statutes, and you will keep My judgments.*" They have no conception of how, to a heart fully surrendered and given over to Christ alone, He will make possible what otherwise appears beyond our reach: loving Him, keeping His commandments, abiding in His love.

The wonderful promise of the Holy Spirit as the power of Christ's life in them was the pledge that they would indeed love Him and keep His words. That was to be the great secret of abiding in Christ, of having the indwelling of Christ and of God, and of the divine efficacy of their prayer to bring down God's blessing on all their work.

The Promise of the Spirit

It is to your advantage that I go away; for if I do not go away, the Helper will not come to you; but if I depart, I will send Him to you. He will glorify Me, for He will take of what is Mine and declare it to you.

John 16:7, 14

THE crucified Christ was to be glorified on the throne of heaven. And out of that glory He would send down the Holy Spirit into the hearts of His disciples to glorify Him in them. The Spirit of the crucified and glorified Christ would be their life in fellowship with Him and their power for His service. The Spirit comes to us as the Spirit of the divine glory; as such we are to welcome Him and yield ourselves absolutely to His leading.

Yes, the Spirit that searches the deep things of God, that dwells in the very roots of the Divine Being, that had been with Christ through all His life and in His death upon the cross, this one, the Spirit of the Father and the Son, was to come and dwell in them and make them the conscious possessors of the presence of the glorified Christ. It was this blessed Spirit who was to be their power for a life of loving obedience, to be their Teacher and Leader in praying down from heaven the blessing that they needed. And it was in His power that they were to conquer God's enemies and carry the gospel to the ends of the world.

It is this Spirit of God and of Christ that the church lacks so sadly; it is this Spirit she grieves so unceasingly. It is owing to this that her work is so often feeble and fruitless. And what can be the reason for this?

The Spirit is God. As God He claims possession of our whole being. We have thought too much of Him as our *help* in the Christian life; we have not known that heart and life are to be entirely and unceasingly under His control; we are to be led by the Spirit every day and every hour. In His power our life is to be a direct and continual abiding in the love and fellowship of Jesus. No wonder that we have not believed in the great promise that, in a love that keeps the commandments, we can always abide in Christ's love. No wonder that we have not the courage to believe that Christ's mighty power will work in us and through us. No wonder that His divine prayer-promises are beyond our reach. The Spirit that searches the deep things of God claims the very depths of our being, there to reveal Christ as Lord and Ruler.

The promise waits for its fulfillment in our life: "*He will glorify Me, for He will take of what is Mine and declare it to you.*" Let us this very day yield ourselves to believe the promise at once and with our whole heart. Christ waits to make it true.

In Christ

*At that day you will know that I am in My Father, and you
in Me, and I in you.*

John 14:20

OUR Lord had spoken of His life in the Father:
"Believe Me that I *am* in the Father and the Father
in Me" (14:11). He and the Father were not two persons
next to each other they were in each other. Though on
earth as man, He lived in the Father. All He did was what
the Father did in Him.

This divine life of heaven, of Christ in God and God
in Christ, is the picture and the pledge of what our life
in Christ is to be here upon earth. It is in the very nature
of the divine life that the Son is in the Father. Even so
we must know and ever live in the faith that we are in
Christ. Then we shall learn that even as the Father worked
in Christ, so Christ will also work in us if we but believe
that we are in Him and yield ourselves to His power.

And even as the Son waited on. the Father and the
Father worked through Him, so the disciples would
make known to Him in prayer what they wanted done
on earth and He would do it. Their life in Him was to
be the reflection of His life in the Father. As the Father
worked in Him, because He lived in the Father, so Christ
would work in them as they lived in Him.

But this would not be until the Holy Spirit came. It
was for this they had to wait until they were endued with

the power from on high. It was for this that they would abide in Him by daily fellowship and prayer, that He might so do in them the greater works He had promised.

How little the church understands that the secret of her power is to be found in nothing less than where Christ found it, abiding in the Father and His love. How little ministers understand that they are to make this their one great object: daily and hourly to abide in Christ as the only possible way of being fitted and used by Him in the great work of winning souls to Him. If anyone asks what the lost secret of the pulpit is, we have it here: "*At that day*"—when the Spirit fills your heart—"you will know that I am in My Father, and you in Me."

Blessed Lord, we beseech You, teach us to surrender ourselves unreservedly to the Holy Spirit; and so daily, above everything, to wait for His teaching that we too may know the blessed secret that as *You are in the Father, and the Father works through You, so we are in You, and You work through us.*

Gracious Lord, we beseech You humbly and fervently, be pleased to pour down upon all Your children who are seeking to work for You such a spirit of grace and of supplication that we may not rest until we too are filled with the Holy Spirit.

Abiding in Christ

Abide in Me, and I in you.

John 15:4

WHAT our Lord had taught in John 14, of our union with Him in the likeness of His being in the Father, He seeks to enforce and illustrate by the wonderful parable of the branch and the vine. And all for the sake of bringing home to the apostles, and to all His servants in the gospel, the absolute necessity of a life, daily in full communion with Him. *"Abide in Me."*

On the one hand He points to Himself and to the Father: Just as truly and fully as I am in the Father, *so you are in Me*; and then, pointing to the vine: Just as truly as the branch is in the vine, you *are in Me*. And now, just as the Father abides in Me, and works in Me, and I work out what He works in Me; and just as truly as the branch abides in the vine and the vine gives its life and strength to the branch, and the branch receives it and puts it forth in fruit—even so do *you* abide in Me and receive My strength; and I will work with an almighty power My work in you and through you. Abide in Me!

Dear child of God, you have often meditated on this blessed passage. But do you not feel how much there is still to learn if you are to have Christ's almighty power working in you as He would wish you to have? The great need is to take time in waiting on the Lord Jesus in the power of His Spirit until these two great truths get the complete mastery of your being: As Christ is in God—this is the testimony from heaven; as the branch is in the vine—this is the testimony of all nature: the law of heaven and the law of earth combine in calling to us: "Abide in Christ." "He who abides in Me . . . bears much fruit" (John 15:5). Fruit, more fruit, much fruit, is what Christ seeks, is what He works, is what He will assuredly give to the soul that trusts Him.

To the feeblest of God's children Christ says: "You are in Me. Abide in Me. You shall bear much fruit." To the strongest of His messengers He still has the word, for there can be nothing higher: "Abide in Me, and you shall bear much fruit." To one and all the message comes: Daily, continuous, unbroken abiding in Christ Jesus is the one condition of a life of power and blessing. Take time and let the Holy Spirit so renew in you the secret of abiding in Him that you may understand the meaning of His words: "These things I have spoken to you, that My joy may remain in you, and that your joy may be full" (15:11).

"Do you believe that I can do this, to keep you abiding in My love?" Yes, Lord. "Fear not, only believe" (Mark 5:36).

The Power of Prayer

If you abide in Me, and My words abide in you, you will ask what you desire, and it shall be done for you.

John 15:7

BEFORE our Lord went to heaven He taught His disciples two great lessons in regard to their relation to Him in the great work they had to do.

The one was that in heaven He would have much more power than He had upon earth, and that He would use that power for the salvation of men, solely through them, their word, and their work.

The other was that they without Him could do nothing, but that they could count upon Him to work in them and through them, and so carry out His purpose. Their first and chief work would therefore be to bring everything they wanted done to Him in prayer. In the Farewell Discourse He repeats the promise seven times: "Abide in Me, pray in My name"; you can count upon it, "you will ask what you desire, and it shall be done for you."

With these two truths written in their hearts, He sent them out into the world. They could confidently undertake their work. The almighty, glorified Jesus was ready to do in and with and through them greater things than He Himself had ever done upon earth. The impotent, helpless disciples on earth were unceasingly looking up to Him in prayer, with the full confidence that He would hear that prayer; the first and only condition, an unflinching confidence in the power of His promise. The chief thing in all their life and in the work of their ministry was to be the maintenance of a spirit of prayer and supplication.

Alas, how little the church has understood and believed this! And why? Simply because believers live so little in the daily abiding in Christ that they are powerless in believing His great and precious promises. Let us learn the lesson both for our life and work, that as members of Christ's body the chief thing every day must be that close abiding fellowship with Christ which always first takes its place of deep dependence and unceasing supplication. Only then can we do our work in the full assurance that He has heard our prayer and will be faithful in doing His part, in giving the power from on high as the source of strength and abundant blessing.

Take time, oh, take time, you servants of the Lord, and with your whole heart believe the word Christ has spoken. Christ asks: "Do you believe this?" Yes Lord, I believe. "Abide in Me, abide in My love." *"If you abide in Me, and My words abide in you, you will ask what you desire, and it shall be done for you."*

The Mystery of Love

*[I pray] that they all may be one, as You, Father, are in Me,
and I in You. . . . That they may be one just as We are one: I
in them, and You in Me.*

John 17:21–23

IN what Christ spoke in His Farewell Discourse He
had especially pressed the thought of the disciples
being in Him and *abiding* in Him. He had also men-
tioned *His* being *in them*, but had not given such
prominence to this as the first thought, *their being in
Him*. But now, in His prayer as High Priest, He gives
larger place to the thought of *His* being *in them*, just
as the Father was in Him. "That they may be one just
as We are one: I in them, and You in Me; that they may
be made perfect in one, and that the world may know
that You have sent Me, and have loved them as You have
loved Me" (17:22–23).

The power to convince the world that God loved
the disciples as He loved His Son could only come as
believers lived out their life of having Christ in them,
and proving it by loving their brethren as Christ loved
them. The feebleness of the church is owing to this—that
our life in Christ, and His life in us, is not known, and
not proved to the world by the living unity in which
our love manifests that Christ is in us. Nothing less
than this is needed: such an indwelling of Christ in the
heart, such a binding together of believers because they

know and see and love each other as those who together have Christ dwelling in them. As we have it in the very last words of the prayer, "I have declared to them Your name, and will declare it, that the love with which You loved Me may be in them, and I in them" (John 17:26). The divine indwelling has its chief glory in that it is the manifestation of divine love: namely, the Father's love to Christ, brought by Christ to us, flowing out from us to the brethren and to all men.

Christ had given this great promise to the loving, obedient disciple: "My Father will love him, [and I will love him,] and We will come to him and make Our home with him" (14:23). It is to live this life of love to Christ and the brethren that the Holy Spirit, in whom the Father and the Son are one, longs to live in our heart. Let nothing less than this, child of God, be what you seek, what you believe, what you claim with your whole heart and strength—the indwelling of the Lord Jesus in the "love . . . which passes knowledge" (Eph. 3:19), with which He can fill your heart. So shall the world indeed be constrained by the love God's children bear to each other to acknowledge that the word is being fulfilled, "that the love with which You loved Me may be in them, and I in them" (John 17:26).

"*Do you believe that I am able to do this?*" (Matt. 9:28). *Yes, Lord.*

Christ Our Righteousness

Being justified freely by His grace through the redemption that is in Christ Jesus.

Romans 3:24

THE first three Evangelists spoke of redemption as a pardon of sin, or justification. John spoke of it as a life which Christ is to live in us, or regeneration. In Paul we find both truths in their beautiful connection and harmony.

So in Romans he first speaks of justification, Romans 3:21–5:11. Then he goes on from 5:12 to 8:39 to speak of the life that there is in union with Christ. In Romans 4 he tells us that we find both these things in Abraham. First, verses 3–5, "Abraham believed God. . . . Him who *justifies the ungodly*, his faith is accounted for righteousness." Then, verse 17, Abraham believed God "*who gives life to the dead*." Just as God first of all counted to Abraham his faith as righteousness, and then led him on to believe in Him as the God who can give life to the dead, even so with the believer.

Justification comes at the commencement full and complete, as the eye of faith is fixed upon Christ. But that is only the beginning. Gradually the believer begins to understand that he was at that same time born again—*that he now has Christ in him*—and that his calling now is to *abide in Christ* and let *Christ abide* and *live* and *work in him*.

Most Christians strive, by holding fast their faith in justification, to stir and strengthen themselves for a life of gratitude and obedience. But they fail sadly because they do not know this second truth and so do not in full faith yield themselves to Christ to maintain His life in them. They have learned from Abraham the first lesson, to believe in God who justifies the ungodly. But they have not gone on to the second great lesson, to believe in God who gives life to the dead and daily renews that life through Christ, who lives in them and in whose life alone there is strength and fullness of blessing. The Christian life must be "from faith to faith" (Rom. 1:17). The grace of pardon is but the beginning; growing in grace leads on to the fuller insight and experience of what it is to be in Christ, to live in Him, and to grow up in Him in all things as the Head.

Christ Our Life

Much more those who receive abundance of grace and of the gift of righteousness will reign in life through the One, Jesus Christ.

Romans 5:17

You also, reckon yourselves to be dead indeed to sin, but alive to God in Christ Jesus.

6:11

WE said that Paul teaches us now that our faith in Christ as our righteousness is to be followed by our faith in Him as our life from the dead. He asks (6:3), "Do you not know that as many of us as were baptized into Christ Jesus *were baptized into His death?*" We were buried with Him, and raised from the dead with Him. Just as in Adam all his children died, so all believers in Christ actually died too in *Him.* "Our old man was crucified with Him" (6:6); with Him also we were raised from the dead. And now we are to count ourselves as actually "dead indeed to sin, but alive to God" (6:11).

In very deed, just as the new life in us is an actual participation in and experience of the risen life of Christ, so our death to sin in Christ is also an actual spiritual reality. It is when, by the power of the Holy Spirit, we are enabled to see how really we were one with Christ on the cross in His death, and in His resurrection also, that we shall understand that in Him sin has no power over us. We present ourselves "to God as being alive from the dead" (Rom. 6:13).

Just as the old Adam lives in the sinner—even in the believer, too, who does not know of the new death in Christ which he has died—even so the man who knows that he died in Christ and now is alive in Him can confidently count upon the word "Sin shall not have dominion over you" (6:14), not even for a single moment. "*Reckon yourselves to be dead indeed to sin, but alive to God in Christ Jesus.*" This is the true life of faith.

As what our Lord said about our being in Him and having Him living His life in us could only come true as the full power of the Holy Spirit is experienced, so it is here too. Paul says (see 8:2), "The law of the Spirit of life in Christ Jesus has made me free from the law of sin and death," of which he had been complaining that it had kept him in captivity. And he then adds "that the righteous requirement of the law might be fulfilled in us who do not walk according to the flesh but according to the Spirit" (8:4). Through the Spirit we enter into the glorious liberty of the children of God.

Oh that God might open the eyes of His children to see what the power is of Christ living in them for a life of holiness and fruitfulness when *they reckon themselves indeed dead to sin and alive to God in Christ Jesus.*

Crucified with Christ

I have been crucified with Christ; it is no longer I who live,
but Christ lives in me.

Galatians 2:20

AS in Adam we died out of the life and the will of God into sin and corruption, so in Christ we are made partakers of a new spiritual death, a death to sin and into the will and the life of God. Such was the death Christ died; such is the death we are made partakers of in Him. To Paul this was such a reality that he was able to say: "I have been crucified with Christ; it is no longer I who live, but Christ lives in me." The death with Christ had had such power that he no longer lived his own life; Christ lived His life in him. He had indeed died to the old nature and to sin, and been raised up into the power of the living Christ dwelling in him.

It was the crucified Christ who lived in him and made him partaker of all that the cross had meant to Christ Himself. The very mind that was in Christ, with His self-emptying and taking the form of a servant, His humbling Himself to become obedient unto death— these dispositions worked in him because the crucified Christ lived in him. He lived in very deed as a crucified man.

Christ's death on the cross was His highest exhibition of His holiness and victory over sin. And the believer who receives Christ is made partaker of all the power and blessing that the crucified Lord has won. As the believer learns to accept this truth by faith, he yields himself as now crucified to the world and dead to its pleasure and pride, its lusts and self-pleasing. He learns that the mystery of the cross, as the crucified Lord reveals its power in him, opens the entrance into the fullest fellowship with Christ and the conformity to His sufferings. And so he learns, in the full depth of its meaning, what the Word has said: "Christ crucified . . . the power of God, and the wisdom of God" (1 Cor. 23–24). He grows into a fuller apprehension of the blessedness of daring to say: "*I have been crucified with Christ; it is no longer I who live, but Christ [the crucified] lives in me.*"

Oh the blessedness of the power of the God-given faith that enables a man to live all the day counting himself, and yielding himself to God, as indeed dead to sin and alive to God in Christ Jesus.

The Faith Life

*The life which I now live in the flesh I live by faith in the
Son of God, who loved me and gave Himself for me.*

Galatians 2:20

IF we ask Paul what he meant by saying that he no
longer lives, but that Christ lives in him, or inquire
what now is his part in living that life, he gives us
the answer: "The life which I now live in the flesh [is a
life of] faith in the Son of God, who loved me and gave
Himself for me." His whole life, day by day and all
the day, was an unceasing faith in the wonderful love
that had given itself for him. Faith was the power
that possessed and permeated his whole being and
his every action.

Here we have the simple but full statement of what
the secret of the true Christian life is. It is not faith only
in certain promises of God, or in certain blessings that
we receive from Christ. It is a faith that has got a vision
of how entirely Christ gives Himself to the soul to be,
in the very deepest and fullest sense of the word, his life
and all that that implies for every moment of the day. As
essential as continuous breathing is to the support of our
physical life, so is the unceasing faith in which the soul
trusts Christ and counts upon Him to maintain the life
of the Spirit within us. Faith ever rests on that infinite
love in which Christ gave Himself wholly for us, to be
ours in the deepest meaning of the word and to live His

life over again in us. In virtue of His divine omnipresence, whereby He fills all things, He can be to each what He is to all, a complete and perfect Savior, an abiding Guest, in very deed taking charge and maintaining our life in us and for us, as if each of us were the only one in whom He lives. *Just as truly as the Father lived in Him, and worked in Him all that He was to work out, just as truly will Christ live and work in each one of us.* (As a living testimony to this, see the booklet *The Life That Wins*, by Dr. Charles Trumbull.)

Faith, led and taught by God's Holy Spirit, gets such a confidence in the omnipotence and the omnipresence of Christ that it carries in the depth of the heart the abiding unbroken assurance all the day: He who loved me and gave Himself for me, He lives in me; He is in very deed my life and my all. "*I can do all things through Christ who strengthens me*" (Phil. 4:13). May God reveal to us that inseparable union between Christ and us in which the consciousness of Christ's presence may become as natural to us as the consciousness of our existence.

Full Consecration

Yet indeed I also count all things loss for the excellence of the knowledge of Christ Jesus my Lord.

Philippians 3:8

IN studying the promises Jesus gave to His disciples in the last night, the question comes, "What was it that made just these men fit and worthy of the high honor of being baptized with the Holy Spirit from heaven?" The answer is simple. When Christ called them, they forsook all and followed Him. They denied themselves, even to the hating of their own life, and gave themselves to obey His commands. They followed Him to Calvary, and amid its suffering and death their hearts clung to Him alone. It was this that prepared them for receiving a share in His resurrection life, thereby becoming fitted here on earth to be filled with that Spirit, even as Christ received the fullness of the Spirit from the Father in glory.

Just as Jesus Christ had to sacrifice all to be wholly an offering to God, so all His people, from Abraham and Jacob and Joseph downward to His twelve disciples, have had to be men who had given up all to follow the divine leading, and lived separated unto God, before the divine power could fulfill His purposes through them.

It was thus with Paul too. To count all things but loss for Christ was the keynote of His life, as it must be also of ours if we are to share fully in the power of His resurrection. But how little the church understands that we have been entirely redeemed from the world, to live wholly and only for God and His love. As the merchant-man who found the treasure in the field had to sell all he had to purchase it (see Matt. 13:45–46), Christ claims the whole heart and the whole life and the whole strength if we are indeed to share with Him in the victory through the power of the Holy Spirit. The law of the kingdom is unchangeable: *all things loss for the excellency of the knowledge of Christ Jesus my Lord.*

The disciples had to spend years with Christ to be prepared for Pentecost. Christ calls us to walk every day in the closest union with Himself to abide in Him without ceasing, and so to live as those who are not their own but wholly His. It is in this we shall find the path to the fullness of the Spirit.

Let our faith boldly believe that such a life is meant for us. Let our heart's fervent desire reach out after nothing less than this. Let us love the Lord our God and Christ our Savior with our whole heart. We shall be more than conquerors through Him that loved us.

Entire Sanctification

*Now may the God of peace Himself sanctify you completely;
and may your whole spirit, soul, and body be preserved
blameless at the coming of our Lord Jesus Christ. He who
calls you is faithful, who also will do it.*

First Thessalonians 5:23–24

WHAT a promise! One would expect to see all
God's children clinging to it, claiming its
fulfillment. Alas, unbelief does not know what to
think of it, and but few count it their treasure and joy.

Just listen. God, the God of peace—the peace He
made by the blood of the cross, the peace that passes
all understanding, keeping our hearts and thoughts in
Christ Jesus—none other but Himself can and will do
it. This God of peace *Himself* promises to sanctify us—to
sanctify us wholly—in Christ our sanctification, in the
sanctification of the Spirit. It is God who is doing the
work. It is in close, personal fellowship with God Himself
that we become holy.

Ought not each of us rejoice with exceeding joy
at the prospect? But it is as if the promise is too great,
and so it is repeated and amplified. *May your spirit*—
the inmost part of man's being, created for fellowship
with God—*and your soul*—the seat of the life and all
its powers—*and body*—through which sin entered, in
which sin proved its power even unto death, but which
has been redeemed in Christ: *may spirit, soul, and body*

be preserved entire, without blame at the coming of our Lord Jesus Christ.

To prevent the possibility of any misconception, as if it is too great to be literally true, the words are added: "*He who calls you is faithful, who also will do it.*" Yes, He has said: "I the Lord have spoken it; and I, in Christ and through the Holy Spirit, will do it." All that He asks is that we shall come and abide in close fellowship with Himself every day. As the heat of the sun shines on the body and warms it, the fire of His holiness will burn in us and make us holy. Child of God, beware of unbelief. It dishonors God; it robs your soul of its heritage. Take refuge in the word: "He who calls you is faithful, who also will do it." Let every thought of your high and holy calling wake the response: ""He who calls you is faithful, who also will do it." Yes, He will do it; and He will give me grace so to abide in His nearness that I can ever be under the cover of His perfect peace, and of the holiness which He alone can give. O my soul, *He will do it.*

"All things *are* possible to him who believes" (Mark 9:23). *I believe, Lord; help my unbelief.*

The Exceeding Greatness
of His Power

*[I] do not cease to give thanks for you, making mention of
you in my prayers: that the God of our Lord Jesus Christ, the
Father of glory, may give to you the spirit of wisdom and revelation . . . the eyes of your understanding being enlightened;
that you may know . . . what is the exceeding greatness of
His power toward us who believe, according to the working
of His mighty power which He worked in Christ when He
raised Him from the dead.*

Ephesians 1:16–20

HERE we have again one of the great texts in regard
to which faith has to be exercised—words that will
make our faith large and strong and bold. Paul is writing
to men who had been sealed with the Holy Spirit. And
yet he felt the need of unceasing prayer for the enlighten-
ing of the Spirit, that they might know in truth what the
mighty power of God was that was working in them. It
was nothing less than the very same power, the working
of the strength of His might, by which He raised Christ
from the dead.

Christ died on the tree under the weight of the sin
of the world and its curse. When He descended into
the grave it was under the weight of all that sin, and the
power of that death which had apparently mastered Him.
What a mighty working of the power of God, to raise
that Man out of the grave to the power and the glory of
His throne. And now it is that very same power, in the

exceeding greatness of it toward us who believe, that, by the teaching of the Holy Spirit, we are to know as working in us every day of our life. The Lord who said to Abraham, "I *am* Almighty God. . . . Is anything too hard for the LORD?" (Gen. 17:1; 18:14), comes to us with the message that what He did, not only in Abraham but in Christ Jesus, *is the pledge of what He is doing every moment in our hearts and will do effectively if we but learn to trust Him.*

It is by that almighty power that the risen and exalted Christ can be revealed in our hearts as our life and our strength. How little believers believe this! Oh, let us cry to God, let us trust God for His Holy Spirit to enable us to claim nothing less every day than the exceeding greatness of this resurrection power working in us.

And let us very specially pray for all believers around us and throughout the church that they may have their eyes opened to the wonderful vision of God's almighty resurrection power working in them. And let ministers, like Paul, make this a matter of continual intercession for those among whom they labor. What a difference it would make in their ministry, the unceasing prayer for the Spirit to reveal the power that dwells and works in them.

The Indwelling Christ

That Christ may dwell in your hearts through faith.
Ephesians 3:17

THE great privilege that separated Israel from other nations was this: They had God dwelling in their midst. His home was in the Holiest of All, in the tabernacle and the temple. The New Testament, however, covers the dispensation of the indwelling God in the *heart* of His people. As Christ said, "He who has My commandments and keeps them, it is he who loves Me. And he who loves Me will be loved by My Father, and I will love him . . . and we will come unto him, and make our abode with him" (see John 14:21, 23). This is what Paul speaks of as "the riches of the glory of this mystery among the Gentiles: which is Christ in you, the hope of glory" (Col. 1:27). Or, as he says of himself, "Christ lives in me" (Gal. 2:20).

The gospel—the dispensation of the *indwelling* Christ. How few Christians there are who believe or experience it! Come and let us listen to Paul's teaching as to the way into the experience of this crowning blessing of the Christian life.

1. "*I bow my knees to the Father . . . that He would grant you*" (Eph. 3:14, 16). The blessing must come from the Father to the supplicant on the bended knee, for himself or for those for whom he labors. It is to be found in much prayer.

2.   "*That He would grant you, according to the riches of His glory*"—something very special and divine—"*to be strengthened with might through His Spirit in the inner man*" (Eph. 3:16) to separate from sin and the world, to yield to Christ as Lord and Master, and to live that life of love to Christ and the keeping of His commandments to which the promise has been given: "[The Father and I] will come to him and make Our home with him" (John 14:23).

3.   "*That Christ may dwell in your hearts through faith*" (Eph. 3:17). It is in the very nature of Christ, in His divine omnipresence and love, to long for the heart to dwell in. As faith sees this and bows the knee and pleads with God for this great blessing, it receives grace to believe that the prayer is answered; and thus faith accepts the wonderful gift, so long thirsted for—Christ dwelling in the heart by faith.

4.   "*That you, being rooted and grounded in love . . . may be filled with all the fullness of God*" (3:17, 19), as far as it is possible for man to experience it.

Child of God, feed on the words the Holy Spirit has given here. Meditate, with strong desire and childlike faith, on what the Father, and the Son, and the Holy Spirit have undertaken to work in you. Hold fast the confident assurance that God will do abundantly above what we can ask or think.

Christ speaks to you: "According to your faith let it be to you" (Matt. 9:29).

Christian Perfection

The God of peace . . . make you complete in every good work to do His will, working in you what is well pleasing in His sight, through Jesus Christ.

Hebrews 13:20–21

PREPARE your heart, my reader, for a large and strong faith—able again to take in one of those promises of God as high above all our thoughts as the heaven is above the earth.

You know what a wonderful exposition we have in the epistle to the Hebrews of that eternal redemption which Christ our great High Priest, the Mediator of the new covenant, worked out for us through the shedding of His precious blood. The writer of the epistle closes his whole argument and all its deep spiritual teaching with the benediction: "The God of peace"—listen—"make you complete in every good work to do His will." Does not that include everything? Can we desire more? Yes, listen—"working in you what is well-pleasing in His sight," and that through Jesus Christ.

The great thought here is that all that Christ had wrought out for our redemption, and all that God had done in raising Him from the dead, was just with the one object that He might now have free scope for working out in *us* that everlasting redemption which Christ had brought in. He Himself as God the Omnipotent, ever-working, will make us complete in every good work. And if we want to know in what way, we have the answer: by His working within us what is well-pleasing in His sight. And that through Jesus Christ.

All that we have been taught about the completeness of salvation in Christ and our call to look on Him, to follow Him, is here crowned and finds its consummation in the blessed assurance that God Himself takes such an entire charge of the man who really trusts Him that He Himself will through Jesus Christ work all that is well-pleasing in His sight.

The thought is too high, the promise is too large; we cannot attain to it. And yet there it is, claiming, stimulating our faith. It calls us just to take hold of the one truth—the everlasting God works in me every hour of the day through Jesus Christ. I have just one thing to do, to yield myself into God's hands for Him to work. Not to hinder Him by *my* working, but in a silent, adoring faith to be assured that *He Himself* through Jesus Christ will work in me all that is well-pleasing in His sight. "Lord, increase our faith" (Luke 15:5).

The God of All Grace

*The God of all grace, who called [you] to His eternal glory by
Christ Jesus, after you have suffered a while, [will Himself]
perfect, establish, strengthen, and settle you.*

First Peter 5:10

WE know how the epistle to the Hebrews
gathers up all its teaching in that wonderful
promise, "The God of peace . . . make you complete
in every good work" (13:20–21). Peter does the same
thing here: "The God of all grace . . . perfect, establish,
strengthen, and settle you." God Himself is to be the
one object of our trust day by day; as we think of
our work, of our needs, of our life and all our heart's
desire, God Himself must be the one object of our
hope and trust.

Just as God is the center of the universe, the one
source of its strength, the one Guide that orders and
controls its movements, so God must have the same place
in the life of the believer. With every new day the first
and chief thought ought to be—God, God alone, can
fit me this day to live as He would have me.

And what is now to be our position towards this
God? Do we not feel that the first thought of every
day ought to be the humble placing of ourselves in His
hands to confess our absolute helplessness and to yield
ourselves in childlike surrender to receive from Him the
fulfillment of such promises as these: *The God of peace is*

completing you in every good work, and *The God of all grace is perfecting, establishing, strengthening you*?

Some of us have learned in the little book *The Secret of Adoration* how absolutely indispensable it is to meet God every morning and give Him time to reveal Himself and to take charge of our life for the day. Is not this just what we have to do with these wonderful words of Peter, until it be an understood thing between God and ourselves? Blessed Father, in view of the life and work of this new day, my heart is resting on You; my hope is in Your Word: "*The God of peace . . . make you complete in every good work*"; "*The God of all grace . . . perfect, establish, strengthen, and settle you.*"

By Your grace, may this henceforth be the spirit in which I awake every morning to go out to my work, humbly trusting in the word: "God shall Himself perfect you. The Lord will perfect that which concerns me."

Ever-blessed Father, be pleased, I beseech You to open the eyes of Your children to the vision that even as Your Son was perfected for evermore, so You are waiting to work in each of us that work of perfecting Your saints in which Your glory will be seen.

Day 29

Not Sinning

And you know that He was manifested to take away our sins, and in Him there is no sin. Whoever abides in Him does not sin.

First John 3:5–6

JOHN had taken deep into his heart and life the words that Christ had spoken in the last night, on abiding in Him. He ever remembered how the Lord had six times over spoken of loving Him and keeping His commandments as the way to abiding in His love and receiving the indwelling of the Father and the Son. And so in this epistle written in his old age, abiding in Christ is one of the key elements in the life it promises (see 1 John 2:6, 24, 28; 3:6, 24; 4:13, 16).

In our text John teaches how we can be kept from sinning: "Whoever abides in Him does not sin." Though there be sin in our nature, the abiding in Christ, in whom is no sin, does indeed free us from the power of sin and enables us day by day to live so as to please God. Of the Lord Jesus it is written that He had said of the Father: "I always do those things that please Him" (John 8:29). And so John writes in this epistle: "Beloved, if our heart does not condemn us, we have confidence toward God. And whatever we ask we receive from Him, *because we keep His commandments and do those things that are pleasing in His sight*" (1 John 3:21–22).

Let the soul that longs to be free from the power of sin take these simple but far-reaching words: "In Him there is no sin" (1 John 3:5), and "of God I am in Him." And "He who establishes us . . . in Christ . . . is God" (2 Cor. 1:21). As I seek to abide in Him in whom there is no sin, Christ will indeed live out His own life in me in the power of the Holy Spirit, and fit me for a life in which I always do. the things that are pleasing in His sight.

Dear child of God, you are called to a life in which faith, great faith, strong faith, continuous and unbroken faith in the almighty power of God, is your one hope. As you day by day take time and yield yourself to the God of peace who perfects you in every good work to do His will, you will experience that what the heart has not conceived is what God indeed works in those who wait for Him!

"Whoever abides in Him does not sin" (1 John 3:6). The promise is sure: God the Almighty is pledged that He will work in you what is well-pleasing in His sight, through Christ Jesus. In that faith, abide in Him.

"*Whoever abides in Him does not sin.*"

"*Did I not say to you that if you would believe you would see the glory of God?*" (John 11:40).

Overcoming the World

Who is he who overcomes the world, but he who believes that Jesus is the Son of God.

First John 5:5

CHRIST had spoken strongly about the world hating Him. His kingdom and the kingdom of this world were in deadly hostility. John had understood the lesson, and he summed it all up in the words: "We know that we are of God, and the whole world lies *under the sway of the wicked one*" (5:19); therefore "do not love the world or the things in the world. If anyone loves the world, the love of the Father is not in him" (2:15).

John also teaches us what the real nature and power of the world is: *the lust of the flesh*, with its self-pleasing; *the lust of the eyes*, with its seeing and seeking what there is in the glory of the world; and *the pride of life*, with its self-exaltation. We find these three marks of what the world is in Eve in Paradise. She "saw that the tree *was* good for food, that it *was* pleasant to the eyes, and a tree desirable to make *one* wise" (Gen. 3:6). Through the body, and the eyes, and the pride of wisdom, the world acquired the mastery over her and over us.

The world still exerts a terrible influence over the Christian who does not know that in Christ he has been crucified to the world. In the pleasure found in eating and drinking, in the love and enjoyment of what there is to be seen of its glory, and in all that constitutes the pride of life, the power of this world proves itself. And most Christians are either utterly ignorant of the danger of a worldly spirit or feel themselves utterly impotent to conquer it.

Christ left us with the great far-reaching promise: "*Be of good cheer, I have overcome the world*" (John 16:33). As the child of God abides in Christ and seeks to live the heavenly life in the power of the Holy Spirit, he may confidently count on the power to overcome the world. "*Who is he who overcomes the world, but he who believes that Jesus is the Son of God?*" "*I live by faith in the Son of God, who loved me and gave Himself for me*" (Gal. 2:20); this is the secret of daily, hourly victory over the world and all its secret, subtle temptations. But it takes a heart and life entirely possessed by the faith of Jesus Christ to maintain the victor's attitude at all times. Oh, my brother, take time to ask whether you do with your whole heart believe in the victory that faith gives over the world. Put your trust in the mighty power of God and in the abiding presence of Jesus as the only pledge of certain and continual victory.

"*Do you believe this?*" (John 11:26). *Yes, Lord, I believe.*

Jesus the Author and Perfecter of Our Faith

Lord, I believe; help my unbelief!

Mark 9:24

WHAT a treasure of encouragement these words contain. Our Lord had said to the father of the possessed child, who had asked for His help: "If you can believe, all things are possible to him who believes" (9:23). The father felt that Christ was throwing the responsibility on him. If he believed, the child could be healed. And he felt as if he had not such faith. But as he looked in the face of Christ, he felt assured that the love which was willing to heal would also be ready to help with his faith and would graciously accept even its feeble beginnings. And he cried with tears: "Lord, I believe; help my unbelief!" Christ heard the prayer, and the child was healed.

What a lesson for us who have so often felt, as we listened to the wonderful promises of God, that our faith was too feeble to grasp the precious gift. And here we receive the assurance that the Christ who waits for our faith to do its work is a Savior *who Himself will care for our faith*. Let us come, however feeble our faith may be, and, though it be with tears, cry: "Lord, I believe; help my unbelief!" And Christ will accept the prayer that puts its trust in Him. Let us bring it into exercise, even though it be but as a mustard seed; in contact with Christ the feeblest faith is made strong and bold. Jesus Christ is the Author and Perfecter of our faith.

Dear Christian, I pray you, as you read God's wonderful promises and long to have them fulfilled, remember the grain of mustard seed (see Matt. 17:20). However small, if it be put into the ground and allowed to grow, it becomes a great tree. Take the hidden feeble seed of the little faith you have, with the Word of promise on which you are resting, and plant it in your heart. Give utterance to it in each contact with Jesus Christ and in fervent prayer to Him. He will respond to the feeble, trembling faith that clings to Him and will not let Him go. A feeble faith in an almighty Christ will become the great faith that can remove the mountains.

We saw in Abraham how God took charge of his faith and trained him to become strong in faith, giving glory to God. Count most confidently on the desire of Christ to strengthen your faith. Then, in answer to the question that each time comes again, "Do you believe that I am able to do this?" (9:28), let your heart confidently say: "Yes, Lord, I *do* believe." Praise God! I have a Christ who not only waits to give the full possession of the heavenly life and the blessings of the covenant, but a Christ who secretly works in me the faith that can claim it all.

PUBLICATIONS

Fort Washington, PA 19034

This book is published by CLC Publications, an outreach of CLC Ministries International. The purpose of CLC is to make evangelical Christian literature available to all nations so that people may come to faith and maturity in the Lord Jesus Christ. We hope this book has been life changing and has enriched your walk with God through the work of the Holy Spirit. If you would like to know more about CLC, we invite you to visit our website:

www.clcusa.org

To know more about the remarkable story of the founding of CLC International we encourage you to read

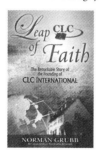

LEAP OF FAITH

Norman Grubb

Paperback
Size 5¼ x 8, Pages 248
ISBN: 978-0-87508-650-7
ISBN (e-book): 978-1-61958-055-8

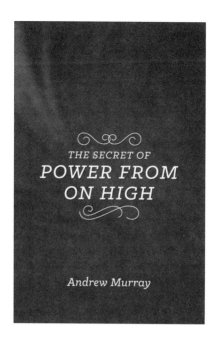

THE SECRET OF POWER FROM ON HIGH

Andrew Murray

Have you learned the secret to a life that is wholly surrendered to the leading of the Holy Spirit? Part of Andrew Murray's classic *Secret Series* devotionals, *The Secret of Power from On High* simply presents how to exercise the great privilege of close fellowship with God in prayer through the Holy Spirit and the meaning of a life of all-prevailing intercession.

Paperback
Size 4¹/₄ x 7, Pages 69
ISBN: 978-1-61958-268-2
ISBN (*e-book*): 978-1-61958-269-9

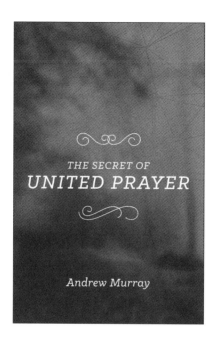

THE SECRET OF UNITED PRAYER

Andrew Murray

Part of the classic *Secret Series*, *The Secret of United Prayer* contains one month of daily selections on the power of united prayer. Murray expresses his desire that many would join the ranks of intercessors—those who pray continually, in unison, for the church of Christ and His kingdom on earth. He studies the "lost" secret of Pentecost: the sure promise that the power of the Holy Spirit will be given in answer to fervent prayer.

Paperback
Size 4¹/₄ x 7, Pages 67
ISBN: 978-1-61958-272-9
ISBN (*e-book*): 978-1-61958-273-6

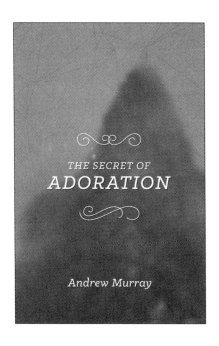

THE SECRET OF ADORATION

Andrew Murray

The Secret Series books contain a wealth of teaching that is based on Andrew Murray's mature and full experience in Christ. *The Secret of Adoration* contains one month of daily selections that highlight the importance of true worship in the lives of believers.

Paperback
Size 4¹/₄ x 7, Pages 71
ISBN: 978-1-61958-253-8
ISBN (*e-book*): 978-1-61958-254-5

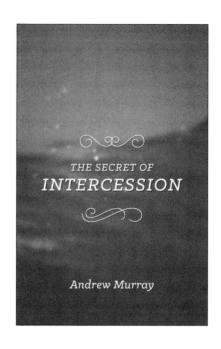

THE SECRET OF INTERCESSION

Andrew Murray

The Secret Series books contain a wealth of teaching that is based on Andrew Murray's mature and full experience in Christ. *The Secret of Intercession* contains one month of daily selections that reveal the power of intercession.

Paperback
Size 4¹/₄ x 7, Pages 67
ISBN: 978-1-61958-249-1
ISBN (*e-book*): 978-1-61958-250-7